VEGA AND OTHER POEMS

VEGA:

and other poems

❖

LAWRENCE
DURRELL

FABER AND FABER

3 Queen Square

London

1973

*First published in 1973
by Faber and Faber Limited
3 Queen Square London WC1
Printed in Great Britain by
Western Printing Services Ltd, Bristol*

ISBN 0 571 10246 8

CONTENTS

AUTHOR'S NOTE

The poems up to 'Envoi' on page 31 formed part of a poetry notebook, partly in prose, entitled *The Red Limbo Lingo*, which was issued in a limited edition in 1971 and dedicated to Miriam Cendrars. To these poems have been added a series of more recent ones for the purposes of a general edition.

THE RECKONING

Later some of these heroic worshippers
May live out one thrift in a world of options,
The crown of thorns, the bridal wreath of love,
Desires in all their motions.
'As below, darling, so above.'
In one thought focus and resume
The thousand contradictions,
And still with a sigh these warring fictions.

Timeless as water into language flowing,
Molten as snow on new burns,
The limbo of half-knowing
Where the gagged conscience twists and turns,
Will plant the flag of their unknowing.

It is not peace we seek but meaning.

To convince at last that all is possible,
That the feeble human finite must belong
Within the starry circumference of wonder,
And waking alone at night so suddenly
Realise how careful one must be with hate –
For you become what you hate too much,
As when you love too much you fraction
By insolence the fine delight . . .

It is not meaning that we need but sight.

NOBODY

You and who else?
Who else? Why Nobody.
I shall be weeks or months away now
Where the diving roads divide,
A solitude with little dignity,
Where forests lie, where rivers pine,
In a great hemisphere of loveless sky:
And your letters will cross mine.

Somewhere perhaps in a cobweb of skyscrapers
Between fifth and sixth musing I'll go,
Matching some footprints in young snow,
Within the loving ambush of some heart,
So close and yet so very far apart . . .
I don't know, I just don't know.

Two beings watching the spyscrapers fade,
Rose in the falling sleet or
Phantom green, licking themselves
Like great cats at their toilet,
Licking their paws clean.
I shall hesitate and falter, that much I know.

Moreover, do you suppose, you too
When you reach India at last, as you will,
I'll be back before two empty coffee cups
And your empty chair in our shabby bistro;
You'll have nothing to tell me either, no,
Not the tenth part of a sigh to exchange.
Everything will be just so.
I'll be back alone again
Confined in memory, but nothing to report,
Watching the traffic pass and
Dreaming of footprints in the New York snow.

RAIN, RAIN, GO TO SPAIN

That noise will be the rain again,
Hush-falling absolver of together –
Companionable enough, though, here abroad:
The log fire, some conclusive music, loneliness.
I can visualise somebody at the door
But make no name or shape for such an image,
Just a locus for small thefts
As might love us both awake tomorrow,
An echo off the lead and ownerless.
But this hissing rain won't improve anything.
The roads will be washed out. Thinking falters.

My book-lined walls so scholarly,
So rosy, glassed in by the rain.
I finger the sex of many an uncut book.
Now spring is coming you will get home
Later and later in another climate.
You vanished so abruptly it took me by surprise.
I heard to relearn everything again
As if blinded by a life of tiny braille.

Then a whole year with just one card,
From Madrid. 'It is raining here and
Greco is so sombre. I have decided
At last to love nobody but myself.'
I repeat it in an amused way
Sometimes very late at night.
In an amazed way as anyone might
Looking up from a classic into all the
Marvellous rain-polished darkness.

As if suddenly you had gone
Beyond the twelfth desire:
You and memory both become
Contemporary to all this inner music.
Time to sift out our silences, then:
Time to relay the failing fire.

APHROS MEANING SPUME

Aphros Aphrodite the sperm-born one
Could not collect her longings, she had only one,
Soft as a lettuce to the sound,
A captive of one light and longing
Driven underground.

Sadness is only a human body
Seeking the arbitration of heaven,
In the wrong places, under the rose,
In the unleavened leaven.

Tell what wistful kisses travel
Over the skin-heaven of the mind
To where an *amor fati* waits
With fangs drawn back, to bleed
Whoever she can find.

But vines lay no eggs, honey,
And even apostles come to their senses
Sooner or later you may find.
The three Themes of this witchcraft
Are roses, faeces and vampires.
May they bring you a level mind.

A WINTER OF VAMPIRES

From a winter of vampires he selects one,
Takes her to a dark house, undresses her:
It is not at all how the story-books say
But another kind of reversed success.
A transaction where the words themselves
Begin to bleed first and everything else follows.

The dissolution of the egg
In the mind of the lady suggests new
Paths to follow, less improbable victories,
Just as illusory as the old, I fear.
Well, but when the embraces go astray,
When you finger the quick recipes
Of every known suggestion, why,
The whole prosperity of the flesh may be in
    question.

PISTOL WEATHER

About loving, and such kindred matters
You could be beguiling enough;
Delicacy, constancy and depth –
We examined every artificial prison,
And all with the necessary sincerity, yes.

Some languages have little euphemisms
Which modify suddenly one's notions,
Alter one's whole way of adoring:
Such as your character for 'death',
Which reads simply 'A stepping forever
Into a whiteness without remission.'
With no separation-anxiety I presume?

Surely to love is to coincide a little?
And after I contracted your own mightier
Loneliness, I became really ill myself.
But grateful for the thorny knowledge of you;
And thank you for the choice of time and place.

I would perhaps have asked you away
To my house by the sea, to revive us both,
In absolute solitude and dispassionately,
But all the time I kept seeing the severed head,
Lying there, eyes open, in your lap.

LAKE MUSIC

Deep waters hereabouts.
We could quit caring.
Deep waters darling
We could stop feeling,
You could stop sharing
But neither knife nor gun
From the pockets of mischance pointing;
How slowly we all sink down
This lustful anointing
Ankles first and thighs.
The beautiful grenades
Breasts up to lips and eyes
The vertebrae of believing
And the deep water moving
We could abandon supposing
We could quit knowing
Where we have come from
Where we are going.

STOIC

I, a slave, chained to an oar of poem,
Inhabiting this faraway province where
Nothing happens. I wouldn't want it to.
I have expressly deprived myself of much:
Conversation, sweets of friendship, love . . .
The public women of the town don't appeal.
I wouldn't want them to. There are no others,
At least for an old, smelly, covetous bookman.
So many things might have fed this avocation,
But what's the point? It's too late.

About the matter of death I am convinced,
Also that peace is unattainable and destiny
Impermeable to reason. I am lucky to have
No grave illness, I suppose, no wounds
To ache all winter. I do not drink or smoke.
From all these factors I select one, the silence
Which is that jewel of divine futility,
Refusal to bow, the unvarnished grain
Of the mind's impudence: you see it so well
On the faces of self-reliant dead.

?

Waters rebribing a new moon are all
Dissenting mirrors ending in themselves.

Go away, leave me alone.

Someone still everywhere nearby
So full of fervent need the mouth
The jewelry of smiling: a confession,
Tidemarks of old intentions' dying fall,
Surely that is all now, that is all?

People don't want the experience
Any more: they want an explanation,
How you go about it, when and why.

But all you can say is: Look, it's manifest
And nobody's to blame: it has no name.

Spades touch a buried city,
Calm bodies suffocated by ashes
It happened so quickly there was no time,
Their minds were overrun
The sentry stiffened over a jammed gun,
And waters bribing a new moon are all
The flesh's memories beyond recall.

The voice may have come from a cloud
But more likely the garden's wet planes
A bird or a woman calling in the mist
Asking if anything remains, and if so

Which witch? Which witch? Witch!
I am the only one who knows.

SIXTIES

The year his heart wore out—
It was not you nor you
Distributing the weight
Of benefits of doubt.
A surgeon season came
And singled loving out.
A power-cut in a vein
To abruptly caption stone,
And echoing in the mind
Some mindless telephone.

Prophets of discontent,
Impenetrable shades
It was not you nor you
Nor something left unsaid
To elaborate the night,
But a corn-sifting wind
Was never far behind.
Be steadfast where you are
Now, in the sibyllic mind,
His one companionable star.

It was not you nor you
The year his heart wore out
But cryptic as a breath
One crystal changed its hue;
Thus words in music drown,
Comparisons are few,
Nor will we ever know,
Tellurian loveliness,
Which way the fearless waters flow
That softly fathom you.

AVIS

How elapsing our women
Bought with lullaby money
To fill with moon-fluids,
To goad quench and drench with
Quicksilver of druids
Each nonpareil wench.

How spicy their blood is
How tiny their hands
They were netted like quail
In faraway lands.

Come, pretty little ogre
With the fang in your lip
Lest time in its turnings
Should give us the slip.

ONE PLACE

Commission silence for a line or two,
These walls, these trees – time out of mind
Are temples to perfection lightly spent,
Sunbribed and apt in their shadowy stresses,
Where the planes hang heads, lies
Something the mind caresses;
And then – hardly noticed at noon
Bells bowling, the sistrum bonged
From steeples half asleep in bugle water.
(This part to be whispered only.)

To go or stay is really not the question;
Nor even to go forever, one can't allow here
Death as a page its full relapse.
In such a nook it would always be perhaps,
Dying with no strings attached – who could do that?

REVENANTS

Supposing once the dead were to combine
Against us with a disciplined hysteria.
Particular ghosts might then trouble
With professional horrors like
Corpses in evening dress,
Photoglyphs from some ancient calendar
Pictographs of lost time.
The smile frail as a toy night-light
Beside a sleeping infant's bed.
The pallor would be unfeigned,
The child smile in its sleep.

To see them always in memory
Descending a spiral staircase slowly
With that peculiar fond regard

Or else out in silent gardens
Under stone walls, a snapped fountain,
Wild violets there uncaring
Wild cyclamen uncurling
In silence, in loaf-leisure.

Or a last specialised picture
Flickering on the retina perhaps
The suave magnificence of a late
Moon, trying not to insist too much.
Emotions are just pampered mirrors,
Thriftless provinces, penurious settlers.
How to involve all nature in every breath?

THE LAND

The rapt moonwalkers or mere students
Of the world-envelope are piercing
Into the earth's crust to punctuate
Soils and waters with cherished trees
Or cobble with vines, they know it;
Yet have never elaborated a philosophy
Of finite time. I wonder why? Those
Who watch late over the lambs, whom sleep
Deserts because there's thunder in the air.
Just before dawn the whole of nature
Growls in a darkness of impatience.
The season-watchers just march on
Inventing pruning-hooks, winnowing fans
Or odd manual extensions like the spade
Inside the uniform flow of the equinoxes
Not puzzled any more, having forgotten
How brief and how precarious life was,
But finding it chiefly true yet various,
With no uncritical submission to the Gods.

JOSS

Perfume of old bones,
Indian bones distilled
In these slender batons;
A whiff of brown saints,
An Indian childhood. Joss.

More mysterious than the opaque
Knuckles of frankincense
The orthodox keep to swamp
Their Easter ikons with today.

The images repeat repent repent (*da capo*)
A second childhood, born again in Greece.
O the benign power, the providing power
Is here too with its reassurance honey.
After the heartbreak of the long voyage,
Same lexicon, stars over the water.

Hello there! Demon of sadness,
You with the coat of many colours,
The necklace of cannibals' teeth.
You with the extravagant arch
To your instep, a woman walking alone
In the reign of her forgiveness
In the rain.

Moi, qui ai toujours guetté le sublime
Me voici de nouveau dans le pétrin,
Hunting the seven keys to human stress,
The search always one minute old,
A single word to transcend all others,
A single name buried excalibur in a stone.

AVIGNON

Come, meet me in some dead café –
A puff of cognac or a sip of smoke
Will grant a more prolific light,
Say there is nothing to revoke.

A veteran with no arm will press
A phantom sorrow in his sleeve;
The aching stump may well insist
On memories it can't relieve.

Late cats, the city's thumbscrews twist.
Night falls in its profuse derision,
Brings candle-power to younger lives,
Cancels in me the primal vision.

Come, random with me in the rain,
In ghastly harness like a dream,
In rainwashed streets of saddened dark
Where nothing moves that does not seem.

INCOGNITO

Outside us smoulder the great
World issues about which nothing
Can be done, at least by us two;
Inside, the smaller area of a life
Entrusted to us, as yet unendowed
Even by a plan for worship. Well,
If thrift should make her worldly
Remind her that time is boundless,
And for call-girls like business-men, money.

Redeem pleasure, then, with a proximate
Love – the other problems, like the ruins
Of man's estate, death of all goodness,
Lie entombed with me here in this
Oldfashioned but convincing death-bed.

Her darkness, her eye are both typical
Of a region long since plunged into
Historic ruin; yet disinherited, she doesn't care
Being perfect both as person and as thing.

All winter now I shall lie suffocating
Under the débris of this thought.

SWIMMERS

Huit heures . . . honte heures . . . supper will be cold.
Sex no substitute for
Science no worship for . . .
At night seeing lights and crouching
Figures round the swimming pool, rapt.
They were fishing for her pearls,
Her necklace had broken while she swam.
'Darling, I bust my pearls.'

But all the time I was away
In sweet and headlong Greece I tried
To write you only the syntax failed,
Each noun became a nascent verb
And all verbs dormant adjectives,
Everything sleeping among the scattered pearls.

Corpses with the marvellous
Property of withoutness
Reign in the whole abundance of the breath.
Each mood has its breathing, so does death.
Soft they sleep and corpsely wise
Scattered the pearls that were their eyes.
Newly mated man and wine
In each other's deaths combine.
Somebody meets everything
While poems in their cages sing.

BLUE

Your ship will be leaving Penang
For Lisbon on the fourteenth,
When I have started pointedly
Living with somebody else.
Yet I can successfully imagine a
Star-crossed circumference of water
Providing a destiny for travellers –
Thoughts neither to pilfer nor squander
During the postcard-troubled nights.

How stable the feeling of being lost grows!
The ocean of memory is ample too,
It wheels about as you crawl over the surface
Of the globe, having cabled away a stormy wish.
Our judgement, our control were beyond all praise.
So prescient were we, it must prove something.

Madam, I presume upon somewhere to continue
Existing round you, say the Indian Ocean
Where life might be fuller of
Such rich machinery that you mightn't flinch;
And how marvellous to be followed
Round the world by a feeling of utter
Sufficiency, tinged a little, I don't doubt,
With self-righteousness, a calming emotion!

I too have been much diminished by wanting;
Now limit my vision to a sufficient loveliness,
To abdicate? But it was never our case,
Though somewhere I feel creep in
The word you said you hated most: 'Nevertheless'.
Well, say it under whatever hostile stars you roam,
Embrace the blue vertigo of the old wish.
And if it gets too much for me
I can always do the other thing, remember?

MISTRAL

At four the dawn mistral usually
A sleep-walking giant sways and crackles
The house, a vessel big with sail.
One head full of poems, cruiser of light,
Cracks open the pomegranate to reveal
The lining of all today's perhapses.

Far away in her carnal fealty sleeps
La Môme in her tiny *chambre de bonne.*
'*Le vent se lève . . . Il faut tenter de vivre.*'

I have grave thoughts about nothingness,
Hold no copyright in Jesus like that girl.
An autopsy would fuse the wires of pleading.
It is simply not possible to thank life.
The universe seems a huge hug without arms.
In foul rapture dawn breaks on grey olives.
Poetry among other afflictions
Is the purest selfishness.

I am making her a small scarlet jazz
For the cellar where they dance
To a wheezy accordion, with a one-eyed man.
Written to a cheeky begging voice.

> *Moi je suis*
> *Annie Verneuil*
> *Dit Annie La Môme*
> *Parfois je fais la vie*
> *Parfois je chome*
> *Premier Prix de Saloperie*
> *De Paris à Rome*
> *Annie La Môme*
> *Fléau du flic le soir*

Sur La Place Vendôme,
Annie Verneuil
Annie La Môme

Freedom is choice: choice bondage.
Where will I next be when the mistral
Rises in sullen trumpets on the hills of bone?

ENVOI

Be silent, old frog.
Let God compound the issue as he must,
And dog eat dog
Unto the final desecration of man's dust.
The just will be devoured by the unjust.

ON THE SUCHNESS OF THE OLD BOY

Such was the sagacious Suchness of the Sage
That all of a sudden in his old age
He was uplifted bodily by
A wonderful Umptiousness.
He became Umptious in the highest degree.

A heraldic uproariousness of mind possessed him
And he said: *If so things are, why let them be.*
Enough of the doctors of high degree
Whose rhetoric is the purest road-haulage,
Damn the deep freeze, bugger the cold storage
Of minds as cold as a lavatory seat.
I will just squat here in my umptious extravagance
Until all the extremes agree to meet.

It was another way of saying
That he had discovered the heraldic law
Namely, that while someone somewhere
Weeps and tears his hair with his claws
In some other spot someone is laughing:
And both from the same damn cause.

Look not for reason anywhere; but keep
Revelation for those who least care.
Be umptious if you can, it's everywhere.
Be umptious asleep, awake, dressed or undressed.
The scrumptiousness of Umptiousness can not be
  overstressed.

Is your gaiety fully enigmatic,
Or are you at odds with some bedwetting ghost?
A mouse gnawing at a coffin is not static.
Why do the many never reach the Most?

To decode even the narrow and finite
Stuff of life is to tumble upon answers.
If only space had edges it would bite.
If time flowed more it would melt into dancers.

The best philosopher of the cryptic mode
Is at best a primrose in the carnal mind.
He only discovers what he set out to find.
There is no sense in all your deadlock.
Consider the bees, they are all born out of wedlock.

Enough of this huge fornication rosary,
Wearisome are the great commonplaces.
They have no aptitude for death, agree,
The million upon million non-Umptious faces.

In the days of all our Yore
Folklore was the only Yolklore
Imprinting was the natural sire
Of earth air water fire.
Now to our vapid visual age
We present our whitewashed cage,
The present burns in iron symmetry
With love built in like a geometry.

If cleanliness is next to Godliness
Umptiousness is a sort of Sumptuousness,
Umption the ultimate fruit
Of holy Gumption.
It is not a question of being conscious
Or washing your little white hands like Pontius.

So spake the Sage, disbursing Suchness
Like a fine sow, a more than Muchness.
To have broad canopy with zip and twang
Is the mark of the sage in his cosmic charabanc.

Pain may be relieved so often
By its own intensification.
How well we know those elephant neuroses
Lead to the girls who always dish out doses.
Live the life of a stowaway in this world,
All places, languages or nations,
Old couples clinging together like tired gloves
Images of disaster in a renewal of patience.

Everywhere revisited is only
Half of the real story, for death is free.
The naked runners braked by the soft sea,
A naked silence going on a spree.
Spread it like butter over he and she.

Whole winters long my ape and I
Winnowed and mused, discussed as best we could,
The fake images, the true-to-what effect
To distil the great elixir of the elect,

34

Sorting the perfect from the merely good.
And when at last it died, without presumption,
I wept, but gave it the extreme Umption.

This is my choice now, music and tobacco,
As happy on my hilltop I review
The vistas of a world it never knew,
To which my Umption is the only clue.
Always at midnight when I hear the chimes,
I tell myself while pouring out a drink,
Things are less complicated than you think.
Dreams, therefore crimes, honey,
Dreams, therefore crimes.

THE OPHITE
(for Saph)

First draw the formal circle O
Of the whole oblong mind, as in the snake
Where mouth and anus meet to complete it.
  The onus
  The harness
Of the heartwhole whose cool apples conspire
Against the serpent like all perverse fruit;
Which identify with sin but remain innocent.
  The tree of good and oval
  Soft branch of all renewal
Where the sincere milk of the whole word
First set the gnostic grimly dreaming
To furnish an alphabet of pure dissent,
  Dark night of the Whole
  Convincing to the finite mole.
Warp and woof like magnets coming together
In silence thumbless as a pendulum.
It could be accident. Believe what you prefer.
No advice worth giving is worth taking.

ALPHABETA

Some withering papers lie,
The bloody spoor of some great
Animal anxiety of a poem he wounded
And followed up in fear, holding his breath.
The blood was everywhere, the yellowing inks
Of old manuscripts reproached.
In stark terror that loaded pen was ready,
With the safety catch turned off,
Only the target lacked,
Crouching somewhere in its own blood.
Some hideous animal without a name.
To be called man, but with such a rotten aim!

LAST HEARD OF

The big rivers are through with me, I guess;
Can't walk by Thames any more
But the inexpressible sadness settles
Like soft soot on dusk, becoming one whole thing,
Matchless as twilight and as featureless.
Yes, the big rivers are through with me, I guess;
Nor the mind-propelling, youth-devouring ones
Like Nile or Seine, or black Brahmaputra
Where I was born and never went back again
To stars printed in shining tar.
Yes, the big rivers, except the one of sorrows
Which winds to forts of calm where dust rebukes
The vagaries of minds in silent poses.
I have been washed up here or there,
A somewhere soon becoming an empty everywhere.
My memory of memories goes far astray,
Was it today, or was it yesterday?
I am thinking of things I would rather avoid
Alone in furnished rooms
Listening for those nymphs I've always waited for,
So silent, sitting upright, looking so unowned
And working my destiny on their marble looms.

THE OUTER LIMITS

The pure form, then, must be the silence?
I'd tear out a leaf of it and spread it,
The second skin of music, yes,
And with a drypoint then etch in quick
Everything that won't talk back, like
Frost or rain or the budget of spring:
Even some profligate look or profitable
Embrace – here to imprison it,
So full of a gay informal logic,
A real reality realising itself,
No pressures but candid as a death,
A full foreknowledge of the breathing game
Taut as a bent bow the one simple life
Too soon over, too soon cold; memory
Will combine for you voice, odour, smile.

A FAREWELL

Colours have no memory, friend,
And can therefore prophesy,
Turn whiter than tea-roses can
With whom to exchange addresses
In far away cities for a good-luck goodbye.

Time slips her moorings soon, and the
Surf-gathering boom of candles can retrace
To the whisper of canvas on the sky
A tiller's lug, jerked like some big dog,
The muscle-softening farewell embrace.

Survivals and calamities supported
In thoughts now, no more in words,
Out there on the flailing waters of everness,
The flora of tumultuous oceans around me,
And for company archaic folding birds.

I will seek out now
All the arts of silence and of anger
For many such Aprils have come and gone.
The lines of your palm are always changing
As you move from the unknown to the known.

So often the bountiful hemlock beckoned me,
I guess it would undeceive,
Ransacked the secret childhood of the race,
To pinpoint the groups of fearfulness
And pardon the terrors it could not reprieve.

The dangerous years approach, friend.
You will be lucky to come through whole.
This speck of lead, a word, fired into the mind
Will in its queer way change it
While never seeking to argue or console.

One thing about death – it isn't far to fall,
Its brightness disfigures every silence,
Its reflections splashed about like in spoons
Gives a reassurance to the dusty kiss of stars,
The cold procession of worn-out harvest moons.

CONFEDERATE

At long last the wind has decided for itself,
Skies arch and glass panes shudder inwards,
My shutter croaks and now you tell me
It is time for those last few words. Very well.
Epoch of a whitewashed moon with
Frost in the bulb and the quailing local blood.
Very well; for not in this season will kisses
Dig any deeper into the mind to seek
The mislaid words we have been seeking,
Delegates of that place which once
The whole of suffering seemed to occupy –
O nothing really infernal, a simple darkness.
But because I came both grew abruptly
Aware of all the surrounding armies
So many faces torn from the same world,
Whole lives lost by mere inattention.

MANDRAKE ROOT

Vagina Dentata I love you so,
You are wide as my dreams are long,
Like the kipling hiss of the cobra,
Or the screams of Fay Wray in King Kong.

Vestal of fire lethargic
Whose seminal doctrines extract
The rivets from Caliban's backbone
To leave him less fiction than fact.

Aphrodite Urania we need you
To lighten the people's path,
By the marvellous insights of Crippen
Or the Brides in the Bath.

O precious pudendum of seeming,
We come from the Gullible Isles,
Where the cannibal complexes frolic
And the Mona Lisa smiles.

APESONG

Hatch me a gorilla's egg
And catch me in the offing,
Buckle me to a wedding ring
And make me die of laughing.

Rock me in the XVI psalm
And fill my bowels with honey,
Up in the trees I'll find a mate,
If not for love, then money.

WANT TO LIVE DON'T YOU?

Somewhere in all this grace and favour green
Autumnal in the public gardens,
Sunk on benches between all ages
Under the braying foliage mimeographed
Like the Lord's Prayer for a computer
In this fate-forgiven corner of reflection
The genetic twilight of a race evolves:
Dreaming in codes, you only think you think.
Sweet rainwashed cobbles of old towns
A moving spur on sundials recording.

The roll of drums buried in the soil,
Somewhere a pair of fine eyes looking out
Under a magnificent forehead, but so full
Of an immense and complicated mistrust
Of human ways: very reasonable indeed
I should say, very reasonable indeed.
Our glances lie unfermented among statues.
A hunchback pokes a dead swan with a stick
While children buzz and cannot fathom.

Then, tied as if to a buoy far out at sea
An emancipated municipal orchestra makes
Some shallow confidences to the prams.
This very spot where the writings of solitaries
Limp off, take passage for foreign lands,
Falter to an end, there being nothing left
With which to compare them,
Never looking back. Well then, goodbye.

THE GREY PENITENTS

Far away once, in Avignon, the Grey Penitents
Set up their chapter on a drear canal
For podgy minds to bleed with happiness
Upon the waters of a supposed redemption
Under the orders of twelve concise pigs,
Revealed their goodness like smooth-feathered men.
They tried like later you and me
To find one beauty without sophistry.

                Alas!
I lit a candle for you once
But it was slow to the last match;
The tiny wick, like loving, wouldn't catch.

Nature's lay penitent, I taught thee to fuck;
But winter came and we were out of luck.
'When the pupil is ready the master always appears,
But sometimes after 9 lifetimes of a thousand years.'

Pale students of the Quite Alone
Whose dreams cut to the very bone
Add or subtract the kisses of the mind,
They will not catch, the engine will not fire,
A vestal love no destiny could bind.

Now on the far side of Europe
We suddenly meet far from that faltering candle,
Not guilty like the penitents of laic misdemeanours,
Wishing never to have been born, all that stuff.
And knowing quite well that even without you
I can easily go on breathing.
But why you come back I cannot fathom.
It reminds me of something I once achieved
To love someone at the speed of thought.

Walking the loops of the companionable Liffey
It came to me to think that over these actual
Waters no shadows lie between there and here,
Thou and I, you and myself, the far and the near.
Nor is the remedial therapy of an embrace the
    answer.
Dark plaintiff of the courtly love how wisely
Your reason has subdued the heart's long pace:
And tomorrow we'll be gone to leave no trace.

Perhaps the primal illness which is loneliness
Can't be countered by a stupid candle
Burning however rosy in the flesh
Of a writer's concise and loving wish.

Would you have supposed, with night
Coming on over the thorn-curdled hills
And the snowy dales, that after this long
Discouragement about you I got kind of severed
Even from poetry, and for so many years?
How foolish to make no distinction between the
    two of you;

The penitents must have documented so much
That ordinary lovers spurn, but to their cost.
A farthing dip is all it costs to formulate
A wish that burns a dogged lifetime through.

DUBLIN

Sweet sorrow, were you always there?
I did not recognise
At first the grave tilt of the head,
Or the meek dark eyes.

To share my deepest joy with you
I sought you – but you seemed to hide
Far in the mindless canyons of your love
Which lay for you, like me, near suicide.

That rainbow over Joyce's tower
Was another rare deceit,
Raising once more those vaulting hopes
You soon proved counterfeit.

SAGES

The old men said: to wet the soul with wine or urine
Then stretch it like choice kid over a drumhead,
Tapping on the cartridge of words one might
Encapsulate the truth of something latent
In time, in destiny, in natural lore,
A caricature of simple intuitions. Giving back.
The old men said: you might arrive at last
To pierce behind the mask, for evermore
Match passion and clarity – that hopeless task.

BY THE SEA

Thumb quantum
Thumb quantum
The fingerdrum drubs, the fingerdrum taps,
We rise into the navy sky
The islands booming with skulls.
With her a feast of white figs,
Cold water crystal on sand beaches,
A late moonrise seeming impromptu.
One could happily die here, perhaps one has,
Too little said about these matters.

One almond-eyed medusa nods
Her fine blond Circassian hair
Twisted up in the shape of an acorn.
With eyes pistachio green to grey,
Like an enamel medal of ancient Greece,
But verifiable and kind to touch.

CICADA

Transparent sheath of the dead cicada,
The eyes stay open like a dead Jap,
Financially no spongy parts to putrefy
Simply snap off the scaly integument of mica.
You could make a tiny violin of such a body,
Lanterns for elves, varnish into brooches
And wear by lamplight this transparent stare of noon,
In gold or some such precious allegorical metal,
Which spells out the dead wine which follows soon.

THE MUSES

Time spillers, pain killers, all such pretty women,
Whose tribal name so nearly rhymes with semen.

In dull male dough they infiltrate their leaven,
Which, though the spawn of hell, tastes like pure
    heaven.

Time wasters, food tasters, bachelor haters,
They hunt with the science of the great predators.

In their mad dreams of one-and-onliness
They feel the self-murder of Kant's loneliness.

Critics of Pure Reason they don't reck,
The quivering kiss, the bullet in the neck.

VEGA

A thirst for green, because too long deprived
Of water in the stone garrigues, is natural,
Accumulates and then at last gets sated
By this lake which parodies a new life
With a boat outside the window, breathing:
Negative of a greater thirst no doubt,
Lying on slopes of water just multiplying
In green verdure, distributed at night
All on a dark floor, the sincere flavour of stars . . .

This we called Vega, a sly map-reference
Coded in telegrams the censored name to
'Vega next tenth of May. Okay?'
'Okay.' 'Okay.' You came.

The little train which joined then severed us
Clears Domodossola at night, doodles a way,
Tingling a single elementary bell,
Powdered with sequins of new snow,
To shamble at midnight into Stresa's blue.
One passenger only, a woman. You.

The fixed star of the ancients was another Vega,
A candle burning high in the alps of heaven,
Shielded by rosy fingers on some sill
Above some darkly sifted lake. They also knew
This silence trying to perfect itself in words.

Ah! The beautiful sail so unerringly on towards death
Once they experience the pith of this peerless calm.

SEFERIS

Time quietly compiling us like sheaves
Turns round one day, beckons the special few,
With one bird singing somewhere in the leaves,
Someone like K. or somebody like you,
Free-falling target for the envious thrust,
So tilting into darkness go we must.

Thus the fading writer signing off
Sees in the vast perspectives of dispersal
His words float off like tiny seeds,
Wind-borne or bird-distributed notes,
To the very end of loves without rehearsal,
The stinging image riper than his deeds.

Yours must have set out like ancient
Colonists, from Delos or from Rhodes,
To dare the sun-gods, found great entrepôts,
Naples or Rio, far from man's known abodes,
To confer the quaint Grecian script on other men;
A new Greek fire ignited by your pen.

How marvellous to have done it and then left
It in the lost property office of the loving mind,
The secret whisper those who listen find.
You show us all the way the great ones went,
In silences becalmed, so well they knew
That even to die is somehow to invent.